Published in 2023 by Groundwood Books / House of Anansi Press
groundwoodbooks.com

We gratefully acknowledge for their financial support of our publishing program the Canada Council for the Arts, the Ontario Arts Council and the Government of Canada.

 Canada Council   Conseil des Arts
for the Arts   du Canada

 ONTARIO ARTS COUNCIL
CONSEIL DES ARTS DE L'ONTARIO
an Ontario government agency
un organisme du gouvernement de l'Ontario

With the participation of the Government of Canada
Avec la participation du gouvernement du Canada | Canadä

Library and Archives Canada Cataloguing in Publication
Title: City of neighbors / written by Andrea Curtis ; illustrated by Katy Dockrill.
Names: Curtis, Andrea, author. | Dockrill, Katy, illustrator.
Series: ThinkCities ; 4.
Description: Series statement: ThinkCities ; 4
Identifiers: Canadiana (print) 20220255814 | Canadiana (ebook) 20220255822 | ISBN 9781773068169 (hardcover) | ISBN 9781773068176 (Kindle) | ISBN 9781773068183 (EPUB)
Subjects: LCSH: Community life—Juvenile literature. | LCSH: Communities—Social aspects—Juvenile literature. | LCSH: Neighborhoods—Social aspects—Juvenile literature.
Classification: LCC HM761 .C97 2023 | DDC j307—dc23

The illustrations were hand-drawn in Procreate, fine-tuned in Photoshop, with some brush and ink on paper.
Design by Michael Solomon
Printed and bound in South Korea

 FSC MIX Paper from responsible sources FSC® C013572

For the bakers of cookies, the shovelers of snow, the fetchers of mail, the stoop sitters, tomato sharers and sidewalk philosophers who make my neighborhood great. — AC

My little slice of city living is made all the better because of my neighbors, and I just want to thank them. — KD

CITY OF NEIGHBORS

WRITTEN BY
ANDREA CURTIS

ILLUSTRATED BY
KATY DOCKRILL

Groundwood Books
House of Anansi Press
Toronto / Berkeley

We all live in neighborhoods. They're one of the most important building blocks of cities. Whether it's your apartment building or street, the park where kids shoot hoops or the sidewalk where you drink lemonade, neighborhoods are where we learn about and connect with the world around us.

But in many cities, people don't know their neighbors. Maybe they don't share a language. Or they don't feel safe because of honking, speeding traffic. Maybe people are always in their cars, racing to soccer practice, school or work. Perhaps they think they don't have anything in common with the people who live nearby.

But researchers who study cities say that neighborhoods where people know one another and spend time in shared spaces are more secure and comfortable. They're greener and cleaner. Citizens are healthier and happier.

That's why people all over the world are dreaming up creative ways to ensure their cities are bubbling, beautiful green spaces. They're turning their neighborhoods into places where people look out for one another, eat together, make art and maybe even stage a pillow fight in a local square!

So how are these people doing it? And how can you help create a city of neighbors?

The physical environment makes a huge difference to how you feel and how you connect with people in your community. When your neighborhood has lots of trees and safe, accessible public spaces to gather and play, you're more likely to want to hang out, shop at local businesses and build friendships there.

Sometimes we can create such healthy and caring places in small ways, say, with an improvised dance party or pop-up basketball court in a parking lot. Maybe no one even notices things are changing until they realize there's less garbage in the alleys, more smiling faces, murals painted on the walls or the sound of music in the streets.

It can take a group of classmates to bring a park or abandoned lot back to life, or it might require city government to get involved. It can cost nothing at all or call for a whopping budget and years of planning.

When people set out to improve city spaces with creativity, inclusiveness and a sense of fun, the process is often called placemaking. Over the past thirty years, placemaking has turned into an international movement of citizens who share the belief that people are the experts, and we know best how to shape our neighborhoods.

Placemaking is not a new idea. Early humans marked their paths, settlements and connection to the world and one another with drawings, cairns, inuksuit or other signs and symbols. They didn't see themselves as separate from their environment but, instead, deeply connected to it. Indigenous people are the original placemakers.

When the first cities were built, everything was within walking or riding distance. Community was all around. But as cities grew and cars were introduced, the way people lived changed. Space for parking and bigger, faster streets and highways became the focus. The city was seen as a kind of machine that we live inside.

In the 1960s, urban thinkers like Jane Jacobs and William H. Whyte began to question this. They studied the world's cities, walking and observing neighborhoods, and found that the happiest, healthiest places put people and communities ahead of everything else — including cars! Maybe, Jacobs suggested, cities are an ecosystem — a living organism capable of change and adaptation. We can shape our neighborhoods and they, in turn, will shape us.

During the global pandemic, many cooped-up people experienced the city ecosystem more closely than ever, and realized how urgently we all need inviting and comfortable public spaces. Our well-being depends on it!

But not everyone experiences public spaces the same way. Lots of factors, including race, religion, gender, abilities, age and how much money you have can affect how you move through your city. There can be real barriers to using shared spaces — from high prices and policing to a lack of lighting or ramps for wheelchairs.

That's why the first part of building strong communities is recognizing and embracing our differences and listening to one another. We need to taste one another's foods, hear each other's music, get to know our neighbors and appreciate the fascinating and diverse city around us.

Of course, sometimes it's hard to find common ground. And there might be city officials or governments that have complicated rules and demand lots of paperwork. There might be neighbors who fear change, or who worry about noise and issues with parking.

Often, starting small helps everyone adjust to a new idea. But whether we want to transform a sidewalk or an empty lot, a parkette or a whole city block, we need to lead with one simple question: What can we do together to make our neighborhoods great?

Turning your community from all right to AWE-mazing can begin with something as basic as a nice place to sit. It could be a deep lounger, a beanbag chair or an artist-designed bench like the one on a busy street in Mexico City, Mexico, that looks like a tumbling pack of playing cards.

The Public Bench Project in San Francisco, California, provides a wooden bench to anyone who wants to place one in a public spot. People decorate them with painted hearts or clouds, as well as plant and tend gardens nearby.

The idea is to create pleasant spots where neighbors can meet and chat, wait for the bus or just enjoy the view.

Simple green folding chairs were also an important part of turning once-dangerous Bryant Park in New York City, New York, into the city's unofficial town square. Unlike park seating that's bolted to the ground, the chairs can be moved about, allowing people to make the park their own — maybe pulling two together for a game of chess or setting up a bunch for an impromptu drum circle.

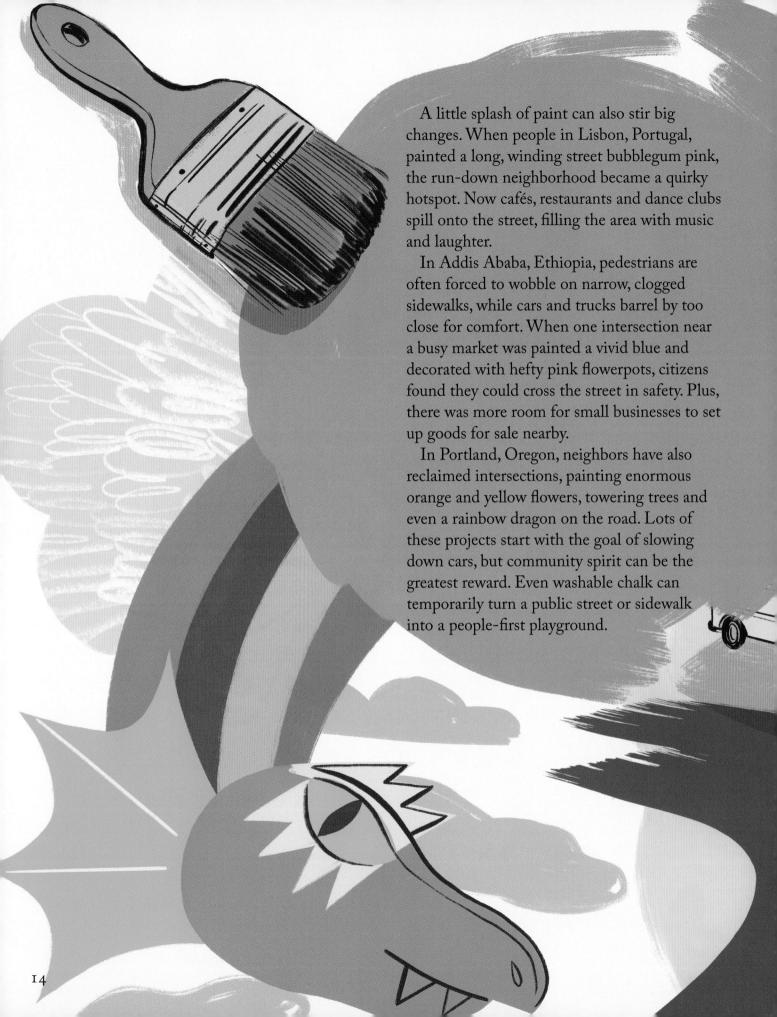

A little splash of paint can also stir big changes. When people in Lisbon, Portugal, painted a long, winding street bubblegum pink, the run-down neighborhood became a quirky hotspot. Now cafés, restaurants and dance clubs spill onto the street, filling the area with music and laughter.

In Addis Ababa, Ethiopia, pedestrians are often forced to wobble on narrow, clogged sidewalks, while cars and trucks barrel by too close for comfort. When one intersection near a busy market was painted a vivid blue and decorated with hefty pink flowerpots, citizens found they could cross the street in safety. Plus, there was more room for small businesses to set up goods for sale nearby.

In Portland, Oregon, neighbors have also reclaimed intersections, painting enormous orange and yellow flowers, towering trees and even a rainbow dragon on the road. Lots of these projects start with the goal of slowing down cars, but community spirit can be the greatest reward. Even washable chalk can temporarily turn a public street or sidewalk into a people-first playground.

Art can work its magic anywhere. In Rio de Janeiro, Brazil, some of the poorest neighborhoods have been transformed with a kaleidoscope of colors and shapes painted over multiple buildings. Favela Painting is run by locals, with young people learning skills and getting paid to paint, as well as repair and restore buildings.

Bronze sculptures like the five boys who appear to be leaping — naked! — into the river in Singapore also surprise and delight urban dwellers. The artwork, by Chong Fah Cheong, is a reminder of the importance of fun and play even in the middle of a bustling city.

Street art can also be a powerful way for communities to speak out about important issues. Within hours of the murder of George Floyd, a Black man in police custody, artists in Minneapolis, Minnesota, began to paint his image and anti-racist messages on walls, buildings, sidewalks and mailboxes. The message was clear — people stood together against racism and injustice.

17

If you've ever turned a corner on a city street and discovered a busker playing a catchy tune or a dance crew performing, you know the joy music and movement bring to public spaces. One artist went a step further, leaving pianos throughout the city of Birmingham, England, for anyone to play. It brought so much toe-tapping, hip-swaying excitement to the streets, the idea spread all over the world.

Mew Mews

In Mumbai, India, two moms searching for great public places for their kids to play decided to make their own fun — and started with music. After weeks of practice, their all-ages choir put on song and dance performances in local parks. Since then, the group has organized pop-up concerts and mini workshops, including a traveling music festival powered by audience members on energy-generating bicycles.

Dancing also brings neighbors together in Auckland, New Zealand, where pop-up local dance drop-ins encourage people to "dance themselves happy."

Public libraries are some of our most-loved and well-used community spaces. Inspired by this, people all over the world have set up box-sized mini-libraries on their front lawns and sidewalks to increase access to books and make their neighborhoods more friendly.

In Tel Aviv, Israel, a group of artists established the open-air Garden Library in the middle of a public park. Aimed at the large refugee and migrant communities, this library has no walls or doors. But it does have two bookshelves holding 3,500 books in sixteen languages! With weekend dance performances and classes for kids and adults, it's become a vibrant hub bringing diverse groups together.

A library carved out of an abandoned building in Petaling Jaya, Malaysia, also helped build a stronger, more united neighborhood. Before the project began, the organizers talked to people about their needs, even asking kids to describe their ideal space using modeling clay and LEGO. Now the library is more than a place to borrow books. People can also do their recycling, hang out with friends, dig in the garden or play badminton.

In some neighborhood parks, toys, buckets and shovels are left out for anyone to share. It's the same idea at Woodruff Park in Atlanta, Georgia, where board games — say checkers or Twister — can be borrowed from a kiosk. Along with colorful chairs and café tables, the games have helped create a welcoming place for everyone who spends time in the park, including families, office workers and people struggling with homelessness. Staff also provide information and referrals for services like temporary shelters and medical supports. This has helped build trust, and the park is now safer and more relaxing for everyone.

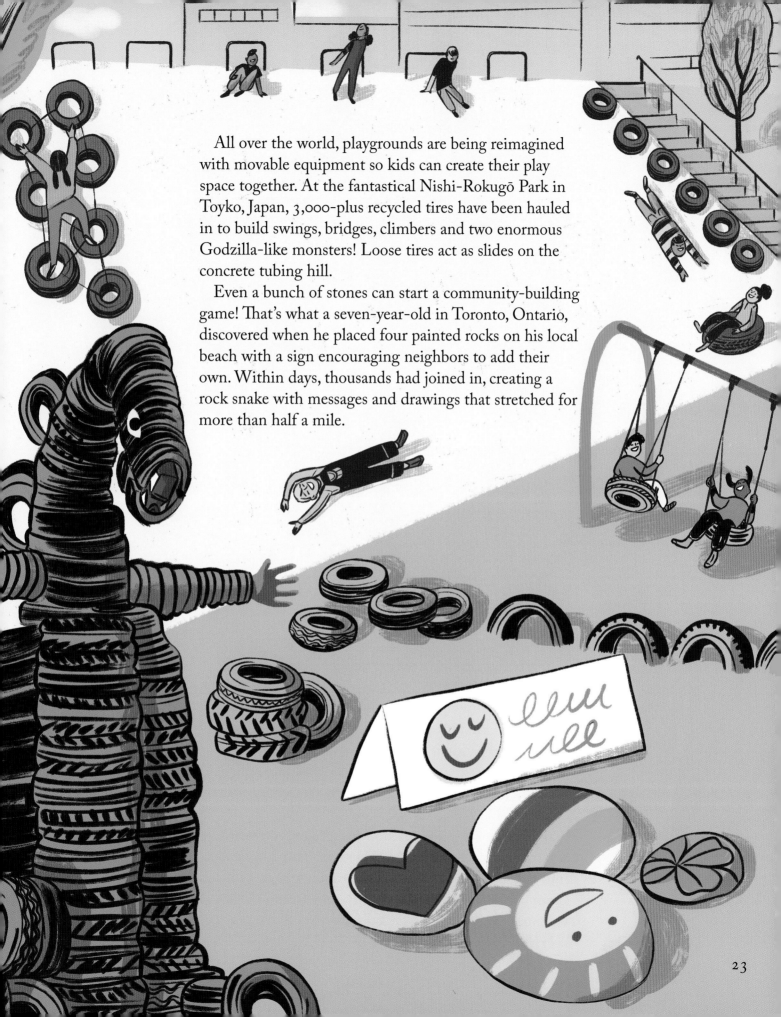

All over the world, playgrounds are being reimagined with movable equipment so kids can create their play space together. At the fantastical Nishi-Rokugō Park in Toyko, Japan, 3,000-plus recycled tires have been hauled in to build swings, bridges, climbers and two enormous Godzilla-like monsters! Loose tires act as slides on the concrete tubing hill.

Even a bunch of stones can start a community-building game! That's what a seven-year-old in Toronto, Ontario, discovered when he placed four painted rocks on his local beach with a sign encouraging neighbors to add their own. Within days, thousands had joined in, creating a rock snake with messages and drawings that stretched for more than half a mile.

Sports can also drive placemaking. About a decade ago, the grounds of an orphanage and school in Nairobi, Kenya, were turned into a skateboarding park. On the weekends, local kids join the fun and can borrow boards, helmets and padding to practice tricks on the handrails, bowls and quarter pipes. Many of the children who skate there say it's the first time they've felt part of their community.

In Seattle, Washington, mountain bikers converted a garbage-covered hill beneath a major raised highway into a bike park with jumps, boardwalks and switchbacks. Once considered wasted space, it's now maintained by volunteer work parties who keep the park accessible to everyone.

Basketball and baseball, of course, also draw people to public spaces. But when kids were asked what they wanted at the Esplanade Youth Plaza in Fremantle, Australia, their wish list included rock climbing, skateboarding and parkour. Now the busy plaza hosts events and workshops as well as concerts that attract people from all over the city.

The sight of sweet blossoms and grasses billowing in the breeze is enough to raise anyone's spirits. No wonder the 400-plus alleys in Montreal, Quebec, which people have planted with flowers, vines and trees, have become the heart of their neighborhoods. Kids bike and play, grow food and spend time with friends and family. Known as *ruelles vertes* (green alleys), they have the added benefit of helping cool the city, replacing pavement with greenery that soaks up the heat of the sun.

When people in New York City, New York, began to transform a long-abandoned elevated train track into a public green space, they were inspired by the wild grasses, trees and flowers that once thrived there. The High Line is now a popular park with many native plant and tree species, as well as relaxing places to sit and enjoy the spectacular views.

Pop-up parks — which might last only a day or week — are another way neighborhoods are turning concrete jungles into community havens. It might be simply turf and a lawn chair laid down on a strip-mall parking spot, or an abandoned lot planted with grass and flowers. These unexpected parkettes can even help increase biodiversity.

Whether it's growing veggies in a community garden, hosting a street potluck or chatting at the local farmer's market, food makes connecting with others easy and delicious. In Andernach, Germany, known as the Edible City, green spaces all over town — from schools to the stretch of land by the ancient city walls — have been planted with shared food gardens. The motto is "Picking Allowed"!

Abandoned lots and old parking areas have also been turned into large urban farms in Detroit, Michigan, where people share the work, and the fruits (and vegetables!) of their labor.

Cooking together can be a powerful force for building community as well. The mouthwatering smell of fresh bread wafting from a wood-burning oven draws a neighborhood together in Winnipeg, Manitoba. Located in a park overlooking the Red River, the mosaic-covered oven attracts young people and families for pizza nights and local celebrations.

The sound of water spraying from splashpad jets or gurgling in ponds also gets people excited about spending time in public spaces. When Berczy Park in Toronto, Ontario, got a makeover, people in the city fell in love with the whimsical fountain featuring twenty-seven cast-iron dogs — and one terrified cat!

Water can even help us feel more calm. In Halifax, Nova Scotia, huge orange hammocks were installed along the oceanfront so locals and tourists could chill out and sway in the salty breeze.

The seaside in Izmir, Turkey, is a concrete, industrial area that doesn't get a lot of foot traffic. That changed when young architects designed simple floating mini-docks that could be linked together. The pop-up docks were a big hit, used by kids and adults to sunbathe and fish, as well as gather for seaside picnics.

Meanwhile, each summer, the city of Paris, France, turns the banks of the Seine River into a tropical paradise by hauling in sand, palm trees and beach umbrellas! People lounge and soak in the sun, swim, kayak, listen to live music and spend time with friends and neighbors.

When a sidewalk, park or square has proper lighting, it feels safe and welcoming. It can also make public spaces magical — from a cloud of purple twinkle lights glowing over a square in New Orleans, Louisiana, to the winter firepits that bring crackling warmth and campfire smells to some parks in Edmonton, Alberta.

In Athens, Greece, one neighborhood decided to make their gloomy alley brighter and more secure by creating a "light ceiling." People donated their quirky old light fixtures and lampshades and strung them up above Pittaki Street. Murals were painted on the walls, new businesses and restaurants opened, and the run-down spot soon became a city destination.

Anyone who's ever been out exploring and realized they need a washroom — pronto! — understands why public toilets are essential community services. They can also be important placemaking tools, because proper toilets and handwashing stations make it possible to spend more time in shared spaces.

When a neighborhood in Accra, Ghana, began discussions about turning a neglected park into a children's play area, washrooms were one of the first orders of business. (Less than half the population had access to basic sanitation at the time.) So the community built low-flow composting toilets, then introduced gardens, a performance space, a library and more.

But even when public spaces have toilets, fear about cleanliness and privacy can keep people away. An architect in Tokyo, Japan, came up with a surprising solution — see-through glass washrooms! When they're empty, you can look straight inside and make sure they're clean; when the door is locked, the windows become frosted for privacy. At night, the toilets light up the park like a gleaming lantern.

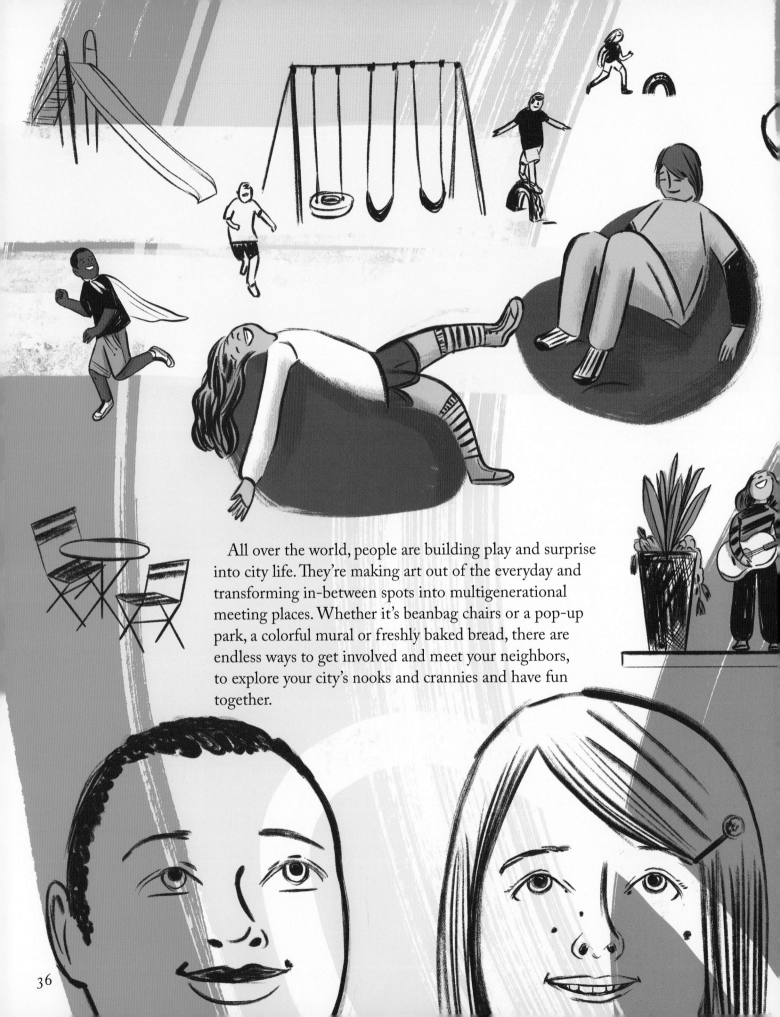

All over the world, people are building play and surprise into city life. They're making art out of the everyday and transforming in-between spots into multigenerational meeting places. Whether it's beanbag chairs or a pop-up park, a colorful mural or freshly baked bread, there are endless ways to get involved and meet your neighbors, to explore your city's nooks and crannies and have fun together.

And the best part is, you don't have to wait for someone else to create the neighborhood you imagine. When we come together to build safe, playful and accessible public spaces, we start to see what else we can do. We start to understand that we have the power and potential to make our communities better for ourselves and our neighbors. Together we can create a place where everyone belongs.

Are you inspired by kids who are painting their intersections and growing gardens in alleys, creating flash-mob dances and building their own mini-libraries? Maybe your idea is big, or maybe it's small. Here's how to get started.

- Define your goal. Do you want to make the neighborhood more accessible for the elderly or more beautiful? Make solving this your aim.
- Spend time in the place you hope to improve. Be a detective and consider how the space is used. Make a checklist:
  - Is it safe and well-lit?
  - How is it used and who is using it?
  - Do people gather in groups or alone?
  - Do they reflect the culture of the community?
  - Are there physical barriers that you will need to overcome to achieve your goal — for instance, stairs or lack of seating or street access?
  - What resources (say, drinking water, an electrical outlet or a shade structure) are already part of the space?
- Gather friends and neighbors to talk about your idea. Give everyone a chance to speak. Bring food to share — eating turns every meeting into a celebration!
- A great place offers many different activities and reasons to stick around. Think about whether the space can offer multiple things to do so many people have a chance to participate.

place!

- Discuss possible obstacles to achieving your goal. Do you need to write a petition and get signatures from neighbors? Should you speak to politicians or business owners? Do you need to fundraise? Can local businesses help out?
- Let people in the area know what you plan to do, when and why. Give them time to respond with questions or concerns.
- Don't be discouraged. This is not only about the result. The process of coming together can be part of the fun.
- Start small but dream big! Experiment. Imagine how you can make your changes last. Can they be a springboard for other community-building ideas?
- Keep track of what works and what doesn't. What have you learned so you can do better next time or ensure your next project works as well?
- Celebrate your successes!

Glossary

Anti-racist: activities, actions or words that resist and reject the idea that one race is better than another or that it is acceptable to treat people unfairly or cruelly because of race.

Biodiversity: the rich and interconnected variety of life on Earth.

Cairn: a mound of stones built as a memorial or landmark, often on a hilltop.

Composting toilet: a toilet that is not connected to a sewer system or septic tank, which breaks down waste naturally, similar to kitchen compost.

Inclusiveness: the practice of providing equal access to opportunities and resources for everyone, especially those who might otherwise be excluded.

Injustice: unfairness or lack of justice.

Inuksuit: structures made of stacked stones or boulders, used as a landmark or sign, often for navigation purposes (singular is inukshuk). Traditional to Inuit of northern Canada.

Migrant: someone who moves from their home country to another place.

Parkour: an activity or sport in which participants move around a complex environment, negotiating obstacles by running, jumping and climbing.

Refugee: a person forced to leave their home because of war, violence, climate change or natural disaster.

Sanitation: systems for cleaning the water supply and disposing of sewage for the purpose of protecting people from dirt and disease.

Selected Sources

Many sources were used to research this book. Here are a few that teachers and students might find helpful for further investigation.

pps.org
creativeplacemaking.ca
thecityateyelevel.com
thecityfix.com
globalcitizen.org
nextcity.org

These illustrated books about community building can offer more insights and ideas.

Dyer, Hadley, and Marc Ngui. *Watch This Space: Designing, Defending and Sharing Public Spaces.* Toronto: Kids Can Press, 2010.

Hughes, Susan, and Valérie Boivin. *Walking in the City with Jane: A Story of Jane Jacobs.* Toronto: Kids Can Press, 2018.

Mulder, Michelle. *Home Sweet Neighborhood: Transforming Cities One Block at a Time.* Victoria: Orca Book Publishers, 2019.

Verde, Susan, and John Parra. *Hey, Wall: A Story of Art and Community.* New York: Simon & Schuster, 2018.

Further Resources for Adult Readers

Jacobs, Jane. *The Death and Life of Great American Cities.* New York: Modern Library, 1993. First published in 1961.

Langdon, Philip. *Within Walking Distance: Creating Livable Communities for All.* Washington: Island Press, 2017.

Manshel, Andrew M. *Learning from Bryant Park: Revitalizing Cities, Towns, and Public Spaces.* New Brunswick: Rutgers University Press, 2020.

Walljasper, Jay. *The Great Neighborhood Book: A Do-It-Yourself Guide to Placemaking.* Gabriola Island: New Society Publishers, 2007.

Acknowledgments

Many thanks to urban designer and city-building advocate Ken Greenberg for generous suggestions and wise counsel. And, as always, much gratitude to the brilliant team at Groundwood Books.